CHEMICALS IN ACTION

METALS

Chris Oxlade

REVISED AND UPDATED

Heinemann Library

Chicago, Illinois

© 2002, 2007 Heinemann Library
a division of Reed Elsevier Inc.
Chicago, Illinois

Customer Service 888-454-2279
Visit our website at www.heinemannraintree.com

Editorial: Clare Lewis
Design: Steve Mead and Fiona MacColl
Picture Research: Hannah Taylor
Production: Julie Carter
Originated by Modern Age
Printed and bound in China by Leo Paper Group

11 10 09 08 07
10 9 8 7 6 5 4 3 2 1

New edition ISBN: 978-1-4329-0054-0 (hardcover)
                  978-1-4329-0061-8 (paperback)

The Library of Congress has cataloged the first edition as follows:
Oxlade, Chris
    Metals / Chris Oxlade.
    p. cm. -- (Chemicals in Action)
    Includes bibliographical references and index.
    ISBN 1-4034-2500 (lib. bdg.)
    1. Metals--Juvenile literature. [1. Metals] I. Title.
QD171 .O97 2002
546'.31—dc21
                        2002004762

Acknowledgments
The author and publishers are grateful to the following for permission to reproduce copyright material: Andrew Lambert pp. **20**, **26**, **32**, Holt Studios p. **15**, Paul Brierly p. **34**, Corbis p. **19**, Peter Gould p. **22**, Rex Features p. **38**, Robert Harding pp. **9**, **16**, **18**, **28**, **36**, **39**, Roger Scruton p. **17**, Science Photo Library pp. **4**, **5**, **6**, **10**, **12**, **15**, **21**, **24**, **33**, **35**, **37**, Telegraph Colour Library p. **31**, Trevor Clifford pp. **11**, **13**, **19**, **25**, **29**.

Cover photograph: of the Experience Music Project Museum, Seattle, Washington USA reproduced with permission of Corbis/Phillip James Corwin.

The publishers would like to thank Ted Dolter and Dr. Nigel Saunders for their assistance in the preparation of this title.

Some words are shown in bold, **like this**. You can find out what they mean by looking in the glossary.

CONTENTS

CHEMICALS IN ACTION

What's the link between an artificial joint, a jet engine, a computer, a battery, and a frying pan? The answer is **metals**. All these things are made of metals or work because of metals, or because of **chemical reactions** between metals. Our knowledge of how metals behave is used in choosing which metals to use to manufacture things, in engineering, in medicine, and in recycling.

The study of metals is part of the science of chemistry. Many people think of chemistry as something that scientists study by doing experiments in laboratories with special equipment. This part of chemistry is very important. It is how scientists find out what substances are made of and how they make new materials—but this is only a small part of chemistry. Most chemistry happens away from laboratories, in factories and chemical plants. Chemistry is used to manufacture an enormous range of items, such as synthetic fibers for fabrics, drugs to treat diseases, explosives for fireworks, solvents for paints, and fertilizers for growing crops.

◀ The light, strong metal aluminum was used to make fuel tanks for the *Arianne 5* rocket.

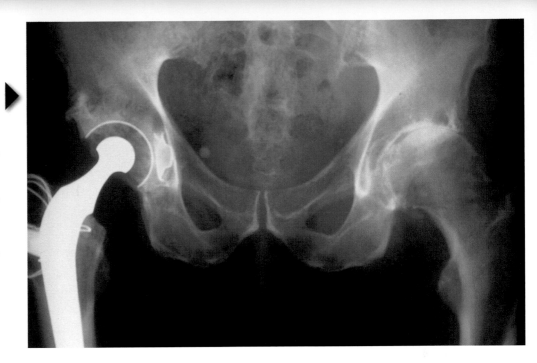

This **X-ray** shows an artificial ball-and-socket hip joint. The lower section is made from a metal that resists corrosion, such as titanium, tantalum, or stainless steel.

About the experiments

There are several experiments for you to try. They will help you understand some of the chemistry in this book. An experiment is designed to help solve a scientific problem. Scientists use a logical approach to experiments, so they can make conclusions from the results of the experiments. A scientist first writes down a hypothesis, which he or she thinks might be the answer to the problem, then designs an experiment to test the hypothesis. He or she writes down the results of the experiment, and concludes whether or not the results show that the hypothesis is true. We only know what we do about chemistry because scientists have carefully carried out thousands of experiments over hundreds of years.

Experiments have allowed scientists to discover many different metals, how metals behave in chemical reactions, and how to **extract** metals from the rocks of Earth's crust.

DOING THE EXPERIMENTS

All the experiments in this book have been designed for you to do at home with everyday substances and equipment. They can also be done in your school's science class. Always follow the safety advice given with each experiment. Ask an adult to help you when the instructions tell you to.

ABOUT METALS

When you hear the word "metal" you probably think of something shiny and hard, such as knives and forks, jewelry, pots and pans, and tools. We make all these objects from metals because they have useful **properties**. For example, many metals are strong, can withstand heat, and **conduct** electricity. Metals are also used on a much bigger scale: they make up structures such as skyscrapers and bridges, and machines such as trains and trucks.

Metals are found in rocks that make up Earth's crust. Getting metals out of the rocks and preparing them so that manufacturers can use them to make objects is a large industry. Various chemical reactions are used to **extract** the metals from the rocks they are found in. Other chemical reactions change the metals when we use them. Some metals, such as iron, are weakened when they react with gases in the air.

▲
The fuselages and wings of airliners are made from aluminum. Some parts are made from strong aluminum alloys.

Metal elements

Metals used in metal objects are either pure metals or **alloys**. Pure metals contain only one type of metal. Alloys contain a metal mixed with other metals or **nonmetals**. When chemists talk about a metal, they mean a metal that is an **element**. An element is a substance made up of one type of **atom**. For example, the metal aluminum (used in aluminum foil) is made up of just aluminum atoms.

Metals are one of the two main groups of elements, and they appear on the left side of the periodic table. About three-quarters of all the elements are metals, and they are identified by their properties, such as their shininess and ability to conduct electricity. The other group is the nonmetals. A few elements have some of the properties of both metals and nonmetals. They are called **metalloids** or semimetals.

Most coins are made from long-lasting alloys that last a long time in circulation.

ALLOYS

An alloy is a material that is made up of a **mixture** of two or more different metals, or a metal and one or more nonmetals. They are made in chemical plants. Mixing different metals and nonmetals produces alloys that have useful properties. For example, brass is an alloy of copper and zinc. It is stronger than both metals and it does not **corrode**.

PROPERTIES OF METALS

There are more than a hundred different elements, and each has properties that make it look, feel, and behave differently from the others. Each element is made up of a different type of atom.

The elements are divided into two main groups, metals and nonmetals, according to their properties. About three-quarters of the elements are metals. They all have similar properties and they are described as metallic. They look and behave in a similar way. Nonmetals are elements that do not have the properties of metals.

This table shows the properties of metals and nonmetals:

Metals	Nonmetals
Mostly solids	Mostly gases at room temperature
Hard, shiny, and **malleable**	Weak, dull, and brittle when solids
Good **conductors** of electricity	Insulators (except graphite)
Good conductors of heat	Poor conductors of heat
High **melting** and **boiling points**	Low melting and boiling points
High **densities**	Low densities
Oxides are basic	Oxides are **acidic**

Inside a metal

All materials are made up of incredibly tiny **particles** called atoms, which are too small to see, even with the most powerful microscopes. An atom is made up of a central **nucleus** surrounded by particles called **electrons**. Each atom is attached to the atoms around it by chemical **bonds.** In a piece of metal, the atoms are arranged in neat rows and columns, and they are tightly packed together. This is why most metals are strong materials.

We make use of the properties of metals in structures such as bridges and skyscrapers. The frame of this bridge tower is made of strong metal girders, while the roadway is supported by strong, but flexible, cables.

Shine and color

All metals have shiny surfaces when they are freshly cut or polished. Many metals lose their shininess after a while, because the metal at the surface reacts with oxygen in the air, forming a layer of **oxide**. Some metals, such as gold, do not react with oxygen so they stay shiny, and are used for decorations, such as jewelry. Most metals are gray or silvery in color.

Changing shape

Metals are flexible, which means they can change shape slightly and return to their original shape. This is why springs are made of metal. Metals are also malleable, which means that a piece of metal can be hammered into a different shape without snapping. Metals are also **ductile**, which means they can be pulled thinner and longer without breaking.

Metal densities

Most metals have high densities, which means that they are heavy for their size compared to other materials such as wood or plastic. Some metals are very dense. For example, a piece of tungsten the size of a large soda bottle weighs as much as an average adult person! There are a few metals with very low densities. For example, sodium even floats on water.

Metal tracks carry electricity across this circuit board.

Metals and electricity

All metals allow electricity to pass through them, so we say they are good **conductors** of electricity. An electric current is made up of a moving electric **charge**, and in a metal the charge is carried by electrons. Some electrons from each atom are free to move from atom to atom and they move through a piece of metal, carrying the charge. Metals such as iron, copper, aluminum, and gold are used in electrical cables and in electrical circuits inside machines, because they conduct the electricity.

In most nonmetals, and in most **compounds**, the electrons cannot move, so they cannot conduct electricity.

Magnetic metals

A few metals are **magnetic**, which means that they are attracted to magnets and can also be turned into magnets. For example, metal paper clips are attracted to a magnetic desk organizer. The most common magnetic metal is iron. The alloy steel is also magnetic because it is mostly iron. The two other main magnetic metals are nickel and cobalt. Magnetism is sometimes used in industry to sort metals during processing or recycling.

Radioactive metals

The nucleus of an atom is made up of particles called **protons** and **neutrons**. Some metals, such as uranium and plutonium, have a large nucleus in their atoms that contains hundreds of protons and neutrons. A large nucleus like this is quite unstable. Neutrons and protons often break away from it naturally, making it smaller and more stable. These metals are described as **radioactive**, because when a nucleus breaks apart it releases **radiation** in the form of invisible rays. Normally the new nucleus has fewer protons, so the atom of the original element has become an atom of a new, different element.

EXPERIMENT: MAGNETIC SORTING

Problem

How can we separate magnetic objects from a mixture of objects?

Hypothesis

We can use one of the properties of iron, which is a magnetic metal.

EQUIPMENT
- iron or steel nails
- copper nails
- brass screws
- magnet

Experiment steps

1 Mix up some iron or steel nails with some copper nails and brass screws.
2 Move a magnet over the mixed nails and screws.

Results

Which nails does the magnet pick up? What do you think this shows about the properties of iron, steel, and copper? You can check your results on page 47.

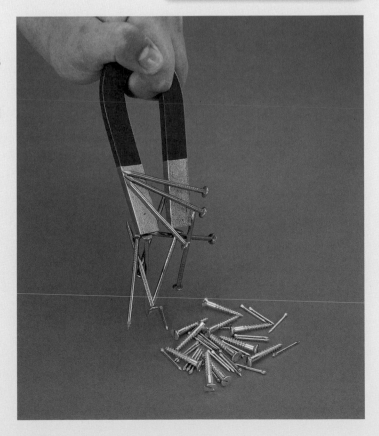

Metals and heat

All metals allow heat to flow through them. They are called good conductors of heat, which means that if you heat one part of a metal object, the heat spreads quickly to the other parts of the object. This **property** of metals has both advantages and disadvantages. Cooking pans are made of metal because they conduct heat from the stove to the food inside them, but if you have a pan that also has a metal handle, you have to lift it with a cloth to keep it from burning your hands!

Metals are good conductors because their atoms are closely packed together and tightly joined. The atoms in every material always vibrate because they have heat energy. The hotter an object becomes, the faster its atoms vibrate, because each one is getting more heat energy. When one part of a metal object is heated, the atoms in that part begin to vibrate faster because they are getting more energy. Some of this energy passes to the atoms next door, making them vibrate, too, and gradually the energy spreads through the object.

When atoms get more energy and vibrate more, they take up slightly more space. This is why all materials, including metals, expand (get bigger) slightly when they get hotter and contract (get smaller) slightly when they get cooler.

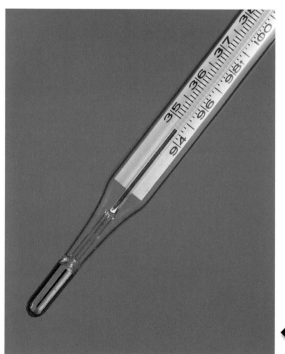

Melting and boiling points

All metals except mercury are solids at room temperature. This shows that they have high melting points. They also have high boiling points. For example, iron melts at 1,535 °C (2,795 °F), and boils at 2,861 °C (5,182 °F). Metals have these high melting and boiling points because their atoms are tightly joined together. Metals with very high melting points are used to make objects that are used in very hot environments, such as inside jet engines.

◀ Mercury trapped inside a thermometer expands when it gets warmer, indicating the temperature.

EXPERIMENT: GOOD AND BAD CONDUCTORS

Problem Are metals better conductors of heat than plastics?

Hypothesis If heat spreads more quickly through metal than plastic, then it is a better heat conductor.

EQUIPMENT
- peas
- petroleum jelly
- metal teaspoon
- plastic teaspoon
- mug

Experiment steps

1 Stick a pea to one end of each of the teaspoons using a small dab of petroleum jelly.

2 Ask an adult to pour hot (not boiling or steaming) water into the mug, and stand the teaspoons in it. Make sure that the peas stay out of the water.

3 Carefully observe the petroleum jelly and the peas, and note the order in which the petroleum jelly melts and the peas fall.

Results

Which pea fell first? What does this tell you about the conducting properties of metal and plastic? You can check your results on page 47.

13

FAMILIES OF METALS

All the metals in the periodic table are found on the left side. They are put into groups of metals with similar properties. These groups are the **alkali** metals, the alkaline earth metals, the transition metals, and the poor metals. This chapter looks at each group and the most important metals in them.

The alkali metals

The metals in group 1 of the periodic table are called the alkali metals. They are lithium, sodium, potassium, rubidium, cesium, and francium. They are called alkali metals because they react with water to form alkaline **solutions**. For example:

$$\text{sodium} + \text{water} \rightarrow \text{sodium hydroxide} + \text{hydrogen}$$

$$2\text{Na} + 2\text{H}_2\text{O} \rightarrow 2\text{NaOH} + \text{H}_2$$

All the alkali metals are strongly **reactive**, and as you move down the group, the more strongly reactive they become. This means they are more likely to take part in chemical reactions. For example, lithium (at the top of the group) fizzes slowly in cold water, but cesium (near the bottom of the group) catches fire instantly when it is exposed to cold air! Lithium and sodium have very low densities for metals and are very soft. All the alkali metals are silvery white in color. Because these metals are so reactive, they are rarely used on their own, but they have many useful compounds.

The alkaline earth metals

The metals in group 2 of the periodic table are called the alkaline earth metals. They are beryllium, magnesium, calcium, strontium, barium, and radium. They are called the alkaline earth metals because their compounds were first found in plant remains in soil. They also react with water to form alkaline solutions. For example:

$$\text{calcium} + \text{water} \rightarrow \text{calcium hydroxide} + \text{hydrogen}$$

$$\text{Ca} + 2\text{H}_2\text{O} \rightarrow \text{Ca(OH)}_2 + \text{H}_2$$

The alkali metal sodium reacts violently with water. The heat from the reaction ignites the hydrogen it produces.

All the alkaline earth metals are very reactive, and as you move down the group, the more strongly reactive they become. For example, magnesium (near the top of the group) will react quickly with steam, but only very slowly with water, and barium (near the bottom of the group) reacts quickly with water. Most of the alkaline earth metals are silvery white in color. Like the alkali metals, they are rarely used alone, but they do form some very important compounds.

The metals in groups 1 and 2 are also sometimes called the reactive metals.

Lettuce seedlings growing under lamps that are filled with sodium vapor, which gives off yellow-orange light.

The transition metals

Most metals are in a large group in the center of the periodic table, in groups 3 through 12. They are called the transition metals, and almost all of them are hard, strong metals with high melting and boiling points, and high densities. The most commonly used transition metals are iron, copper, zinc, gold, and silver. Most of the other transition metals are very rare, and yet scientists and engineers have found uses for many of them. They are mixed with iron, steel, or aluminum to make various alloys for engineering. Several, including palladium and platinum, are used as **catalysts** to speed up reactions in chemical plants.

Two groups of transition metals (sometimes called inner transition metals) do not fit neatly into the periodic table, and are sometimes left out and shown in a separate block. They are called the lanthanides and the actinides, and many of them have only been made in the laboratory. Many, such as uranium, are also radioactive.

The transition metal chromium is used to make shiny parts for cars, and also to make stainless steel.

Gold and silver

Gold is the yellowish metal used to make jewelry and ornaments. It stays shiny because, unlike most other metals, it is very unreactive. This means it does not react with the air to form a layer of oxide that spoils the shine. Gold is quite soft, so it is normally alloyed with other metals (usually copper or silver) to keep it from wearing away.

Silver is a whitish metal also used to make jewelry and ornaments. It gradually reacts with the air to form a brown layer of oxide. This process is called tarnishing, and it means that silver must be cleaned every few months. Many objects, including ornaments and silverware, are silver-plated. This means they are made of steel with a thin layer of silver on the outside.

METALS IN YOUR BODY

Your body needs some metals for it to grow and work properly. For example, roughly 2 percent of your body is calcium, found mostly in your bones. Our main source of calcium as we grow is milk. There are other metals in our bodies in tiny amounts, such as iron, zinc, magnesium, and copper.

It is important to eat foods that contain these metals. Some people take vitamins, such as iron tablets, to provide them with these trace metals, which are found in small amounts, or traces, in the body. You should not take tablets like these unless an adult or medical practitioner says it is safe to do so.

Iron and steel

Iron is a transition metal and one of the few magnetic metals. It is the most widely used metal of all. Pure iron is light in color and quite soft. Sometimes it is made into decorative objects, such as gates, railings, and fire grates. Blacksmiths work with iron by heating it to make it softer and then hammering it into shape. Iron is also made into large machine parts, such as cylinder blocks in engines, and objects, such as drain covers and pipes.

Decorative gates and railings are made of a type of impure iron called wrought iron.

Iron is often made into steel, which is an alloy of iron and carbon. Most steel contains about 99 percent iron and about 1 percent carbon. Steel is stronger and harder than pure iron, but less malleable and ductile. It is good for making objects that need to be strong, so it is used in thousands of different objects, such as cars, ships, building frames, bridges, nails, screws, and knives and forks.

Iron and steel rust quickly in damp air. You can find out how they are protected from rusting on page 28. Stainless steel is an alloy of steel that contains roughly 10 percent chromium, another metal. The chromium keeps the steel from rusting, even if it gets scratched.

You can find out how iron and steel are made on page 36.

Copper was used for this decorative roof. The surface of the copper eventually turns green in damp air.

Copper

Copper is a soft, brown transition metal. It is a very good conductor of electricity, so it is used to make wires and cables. It is not very reactive, so it does not corrode in damp air like iron, and it is also easy to cut and shape. These properties make it ideal for manufacturing water pipes and heating systems. Brass, used to make house fittings such as door handles, locks, and screws, is an alloy of copper and zinc. Many coins are made from copper alloys. The alloy keeps the color of the copper, but is harder. Coins made from alloys last longer than copper ones would.

Zinc

Zinc is a soft, silvery transition metal. Its main use is for **galvanizing**, which is a way of preventing steel objects from rusting by coating them with a thin layer of zinc. Zinc is also used in batteries and for mixing with copper to make the alloy brass.

Poor metals

The remaining metals are in groups 3, 4, 5, and 6 of the periodic table, although each of these groups also contains elements that are nonmetals. The metals appear on the right side of the table (see page 41).

These metals are often called poor metals because they are much softer and weaker than the transition metals. They also have lower melting and boiling points. The most important of these metals are aluminum, tin, and lead.

Aluminum

Aluminum is a silver-colored metal. It is the most abundant metal in the rocks of Earth's crust and has several useful properties. It is only about one-third the density of steel, but is just as strong when it is alloyed with small amounts of other metals. All large airplanes, and some cars and boats, are made from aluminum alloys. Aluminum is quite reactive, but its oxide is very unreactive. This means that a coating of oxide forms naturally on aluminum objects, which stops any further **corrosion**. Most aluminum is made into soda cans and aluminum foil.

Tin

Tin is used to make a material called tin plate, which is steel with a thin layer of tin on one side. Tin cans are made from tin plate, with the tin on the inside—next to the food. The tin keeps the steel from being corroded by the contents of the can.

◀ Solder is an alloy of lead and tin. The soldering iron melts it easily. It turns quickly solid again, joining the wires together.

Lead

Lead is a very dense, gray metal. It is used in buildings for waterproofing because it does not corrode. Thick sheets of lead block radiation, so it is also used to protect staff and patients in hospitals from **X-rays**. Lead used to be made into water pipes, but this was stopped because lead is poisonous and small amounts of it were carried from the pipes into drinking water.

Metalloids

Most elements have either the properties of metals or the properties of nonmetals, although there are a few elements with some properties of both. They are called metalloids or semimetals. An example is the metalloid arsenic, which is shiny like a metal, but does not conduct electricity or heat. Silicon is the most common metalloid—in fact, it is the second most common element on Earth. Pure silicon is hard, shiny, and gray.

The most important use of metalloids is to make materials called semiconductors. A semiconductor is a material that can conduct some electricity (compared to an insulator) but not as well as metals, which are good conductors. This means it can be used to turn electric currents on and off. Microchips, often called silicon chips, are also made from silicon or other metalloids.

Silicon chips are made by building layers of semiconductors onto a wafer of silicon. This photograph has been magnified many times.

METALS IN REACTIONS

The most common reactions of metals are with air, water, and **acids**.

Iron or steel objects that are left outdoors quickly turn brown and flaky. This process is called rusting. The bright white flashes of fireworks are caused by magnesium in the fireworks burning. These are both examples of metals reacting with other substances.

Metals and the air

Most metals react with oxygen in the air to form a metal oxide. Here is an example of a metal reacting with oxygen:

$$\text{aluminum} + \text{oxygen} \rightarrow \text{aluminum oxide}$$
$$4Al + 3O_2 \rightarrow 2Al_2O_3$$

Oxygen is added to the aluminum, in what is called an oxidation reaction. The aluminum is oxidized. The evidence that the reaction has happened is that the shininess on the aluminum's surface disappears—this is called tarnishing. The aluminum oxide keeps oxygen from getting to the aluminum underneath and prevents further tarnishing.

Some metals react with cold air. One example is sodium, which is stored in oil because it tarnishes so quickly in the air. Some metals, such as magnesium, only react when they are heated. Others, such as iron, react only slowly, even when they are heated. Other metals, such as gold, do not react at all—they are completely unreactive.

◀ Exposed calcium reacts quickly with oxygen in the air to form a layer of calcium oxide.

EXPERIMENT: METAL AND AIR REACTIONS

Problem

Do common metals react with the air?

Hypothesis

Everyday metals such as iron, copper, and aluminum look shiny. They do not react with the air at room temperature, but they might when they are heated.

EQUIPMENT
- thin strands of copper wire
- thin strands of iron wire or steel wool
- aluminum foil
- tongs or a clothes pin

Experiment steps

1 Cut a piece of aluminum foil about 12 inches (30 centimeters) long and ½ inch (1 centimeter) wide. Ask an adult to strip 2 inches (5 centimeters) of insulation from copper wire and iron wire.

2 An adult must do this step for you. Ask them to heat the last half inch of the foil in the flame of a gas stove until it glows red hot. Then remove it from the heat. Do the same with the iron wire and copper wire.

3 Allow the metals to cool for a few minutes and examine the parts that you have heated.

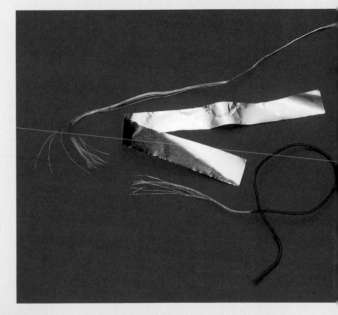

Results

What do the metals look like now? What do you think caused this change? Which metal reacted most quickly, and what does this tell you about its place in the reactivity series? You can check your results on page 47.

Metals and acids

Most metals react with acids. When a piece of metal is put in an acid, the metal fizzes because a gas is formed. The gas is hydrogen, which is released from the acid. The metal combines with the rest of the acid to make a chemical called a salt. Here is an example of an acid-metal reaction:

magnesium	+	sulfuric acid	$\rightarrow$ $\rightarrow$	hydrogen	+	magnesium sulfate
Mg	+	H_2SO_4	$\rightarrow$	H_2	+	$MgSO_4$

The metal pushes out, or displaces, the hydrogen from the acid; this is an example of a displacement reaction.

When different metals are added to acids, the fizzing happens at different speeds. When reactive metals, such as potassium, are added to acid, the reaction is so fast that the metal explodes. With other metals, such as magnesium, the fizzing does happen quickly but not explosively. When metals such as iron are added to acids, the fizzing happens slowly. Some metals, such as gold, do not react with acids at all.

Magnesium ribbon reacting with hydrochloric acid, producing bubbles of hydrogen.

EXPERIMENT: REACTIONS OF METALS AND ACIDS

Problem

How can we remove the zinc from a galvanized steel nail?

Hypothesis

Zinc reacts with acids better than steel; it might react with a weak acid, forming a salt, leaving the steel behind. Vinegar contains a weak acid called acetic acid, so putting the nail in vinegar should work.

EQUIPMENT
- galvanized steel nail
- white vinegar
- glass jar

Experiment steps

1 Pour about 1 inch (2 centimeters) of vinegar into a glass jar. Vinegar is a weak acid, so be careful not to splash any in your eyes. Drop in a galvanized steel nail, and look at the nail every half an hour to see what is happening.
2 Wash the nail when the fizzing has stopped.

Results

What happens to the nail after you put it in the vinegar? What do you think has caused this? You can check your results on page 47.

Metals and water

Some metals react with water. When a piece of one of these metals is put in water, it fizzes because a gas is formed. The gas is hydrogen, which is released from the water. The metal combines with the hydrogen and oxygen in the water to make a hydroxide. This makes the solution alkaline. Here is an example of a metal-water reaction:

$$\text{sodium} + \text{water} \rightarrow \text{sodium hydroxide} + \text{hydrogen}$$

$$2Na + 2H_2O \rightarrow 2NaOH + H_2$$

Some metals, such as potassium, react violently with water, and this reaction makes enough heat to ignite the hydrogen gas. Some metals, such as magnesium, react slowly with water, and others, such as copper, do not react with water at all. Some metals that do not react quickly with water, such as iron, will react with steam to make an oxide and water.

A piece of potassium reacting with water.

The reactivity series

Different metals react with air, water, and acids at different speeds. In each reaction the **reactant** and **products** are similar, but some metals react quickly while others react slowly. This is an example of a **trend**—it is always the same metals that react quickly and the same metals that react slowly.

We can list common metals in order of how quickly they react, with the ones that react most quickly at the top. The order is the same for reactions with air, water, and acids. Chemists call the list the reactivity series. Here is the reactivity series of common metals:

Metal	Symbol	Reactivity
potassium	K	Most reactive
sodium	Na	
calcium	Ca	
magnesium	Mg	
aluminum	Al	
zinc	Zn	
iron	Fe	
lead	Pb	
copper	Cu	
silver	Ag	
gold	Au	Least reactive

The reactivity series helps us figure out what might happen during some chemical reactions. For example, a metal higher in the series will displace a metal lower in the series from a compound, like this:

copper + magnesium → magnesium + copper
sulfate   sulfate

$$CuSO_4 + Mg \rightarrow MgSO_4 + Cu$$

Hydrogen is often included in the reactivity series. Acids contain hydrogen, and will react with metals higher in the series, but they do not react with metals lower in the series. In the series above, hydrogen would be between lead and copper.

Corrosion

Corrosion is caused by a reaction between a metal and oxygen in the air, and sometimes with water or water vapor, too. We normally use the word corrosion when the reaction spoils and weakens the metal. Some metals, such as iron and steel, corrode quickly in damp air. Others, such as gold, do not corrode at all because they are very unreactive. Some metals, such as aluminum and zinc, do react with the air, but they do not corrode. This is because the metal oxide layer made by the reaction protects the metal underneath. This is why zinc and aluminum are used to make or cover objects that are outdoors.

Rusting

The most common form of corrosion is rusting. Rusting is the corrosion of iron and steel when they react with oxygen and water. The flaky, red-brown rust is called iron oxide, and it crumbles away, allowing the metal underneath to rust, too. Here is the equation for the reaction that makes rust:

$$\text{iron} + \text{oxygen} \rightarrow \text{iron oxide}$$
$$4Fe + 3O_2 \rightarrow 2Fe_2O_3$$

Preventing rusting

Rusting of steel is an expensive problem, so it is important to prevent it. The easiest solution is to cover the steel, so that air and water cannot reach it. This can be done with paint, plastic, grease, or another metal that does not corrode, such as zinc. Covering steel with zinc is called galvanization.

▲ The steel body of this van is gradually rusting away.

EXPERIMENT: WHAT CAUSES RUSTING?

Problem

What causes iron and steel objects to rust?

Hypothesis

Iron or steel objects rust when they are left outdoors, but not when they are inside, so it is probably water or air, or both, that cause rusting.

EQUIPMENT
- steel nails (about 2 in. (5 cm) long)
- 4 glass jars
- plastic wrap
- calcium chloride (if available)
- oil (such as cooking oil)
- boiled water

Experiment steps

1 Set four glass jars in a row and number them from 1 to 4. Drop a steel nail into each jar.
2 Pour 1 inch (2 centimeters) of tap water into jar 1.
3 Fill jar 2 to the brim with water that has been boiled by an adult to remove dissolved air, then cooled. Cover it with plastic wrap, which will keep air from redissolving in the water.
4 Put a few lumps of calcium chloride in jar 3. This will keep the air in the jar dry. If no calcium chloride is available leave the jar empty, and put some plastic wrap over the top to keep damp air from getting in.
5 Fill jar 4 with oil so that it covers the nail.
6 Observe the jars each day for three days and write down what has happened to each nail in each jar.

Jar 1   Jar 2   Jar 3   Jar 4

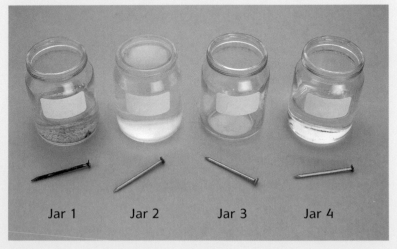

Jar 1   Jar 2   Jar 3   Jar 4

Results

What happens to the nails in each of the jars? What does this show about the effects of air and water on steel? Do you think both are necessary for rusting? Check your results on page 47.

FINDING METALS

All the different metals you see in ornaments, tools, furniture, buildings, and machines come from rocks that form Earth's crust. Before we can use metals, we have to find the rocks that contain them, dig them out, and then extract the metals from them. Some metals are abundant. For example, aluminum, the most abundant metal, makes up 7 percent of Earth's crust. Others are very rare, such as gold, which makes up only 0.0000005 percent of Earth's crust!

Metal	Percentage of Earth's crust	Date discovered
aluminum	7	1825
sodium	2.5	1807
magnesium	2	1755
zinc	0.007	2,000 years ago
iron	4	3,000 years ago
tin	0.0002	6,000 years ago
lead	0.0015	6,500 years ago
copper	0.0045	7,000 years ago
gold	0.0000005	10,000 years ago

This table shows the percentage of Earth's crust made up by the most common metals.

Metal ores

Most metals are found in compounds, which are often metal oxides. These compounds are called **ores**, and they are normally mixed with other compounds in the rocks. Mining companies find the rocks by carrying out **geological surveys**. After the rocks are mined they are crushed, ready for the metals to be extracted.

Very unreactive metals, such as gold, are not locked up in compounds. They are called **native metals**, and are often found in rocks as lumps called nuggets.

Extracting metals from ores

Metals are extracted from their ores using chemical reactions. In a reaction to extract a metal from its ore, the ore is one of the reactants and the metal is one of the products. The higher in the reactivity series the metal is, the more difficult it is to extract it from its ore, and so the more expensive it is to produce and to buy.

Copper ore that has been blasted from a quarry. ▶

DISCOVERING METALS

The discovery of different common metals through the ages is closely linked to the reactivity series. Gold and silver do not react easily and are often found as elements (not combined in compounds). They were discovered more than 10,000 years ago. Copper was discovered next because it is only slightly reactive and can be extracted from its ore easily. From about 5,000 years ago, bronze, an alloy of copper and tin, was used to make weapons and ornaments. Iron, which is more reactive than copper, was discovered next, before Roman times. Aluminum is very reactive, so it is difficult to extract from its ore. Ancient people did not even know it existed, and it was not extracted until 1825. When the electricity supplies needed for electrolysis (see page 34) became available, large amounts were extracted.

Extraction reactions

The main methods of extracting metals from their ores are: decomposition, displacement, and electrolysis. In each case, some energy must be supplied to break up the ore into its elements. All the methods of extracting metals from their ores are also known as smelting. For example, iron smelting is a process for getting iron from iron ore.

Decomposition

A decomposition reaction is one in which a compound splits to make two or more different elements or more simple compounds. Thermal decomposition happens when a material is heated. Mercury is extracted from mercury oxide by thermal decomposition. Mercury oxide is a red powder, which **decomposes** on heating to make liquid mercury metal and oxygen gas.

$$\text{mercury oxide} \rightarrow \text{mercury} + \text{oxygen}$$
$$2\text{HgO} \rightarrow 2\text{Hg} + \text{O}_2$$

Thermal decomposition only works for metals that are quite unreactive. The ores of more reactive metals, such as iron and copper, would have to be heated to an extremely high temperature to make them decompose.

Heated mercury oxide decomposing. You can see mercury metal forming on the side of the test tube.

Displacement

When a reactive metal reacts with the compound of a less reactive metal, the more reactive metal can displace (push out) the less reactive metal from the compound. The more reactive metal forms a new compound, and the less reactive metal is left on its own. These reactions are called displacement reactions. For example, if iron filings are added to a solution of copper sulfate, the iron (which is more reactive than copper) displaces the copper. Iron sulfate and copper metal are formed as a result.

iron + copper sulfate	$\rightarrow$	iron sulfate + copper
$Fe + CuSO_4$	$\rightarrow$	$FeSO_4 + Cu$

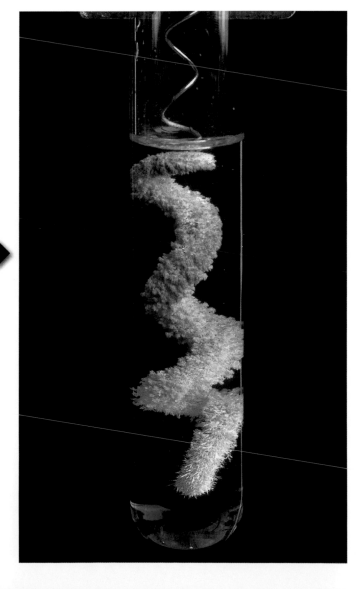

A displacement reaction in progress. Copper is displacing the silver in silver nitrate solution, leaving silver metal.

Electrolysis

Electrolysis is a way of splitting a compound into its elements using electricity. It is used to decompose ores that would need to be heated to extremely high temperatures before they would decompose. Aluminum, magnesium, and sodium are all extracted from their ores by electrolysis.

Electrolysis can only happen to a substance that contains charged particles called ions. If an atom loses electrons it becomes a positively charged ion, and if an atom gains electrons it becomes a negatively charged ion. The substance must also be molten to make a liquid, or dissolved in a liquid to make a solution, because the ions must be free to move around.

To make electrolysis happen, two electrical contacts, called electrodes, are put into the liquid and then connected to a supply of electricity. This makes ions with a positive charge move through the liquid to one electrode, and ions with a negative charge move to the other electrode. When the ions reach the electrodes, they turn back into atoms.

Electrolysis in progress at an aluminum smelting plant.

Extracting aluminum

The main ore of aluminum is called bauxite, and it contains aluminum oxide. Aluminum is very reactive, so it does not decompose when it is heated. This means it must be extracted by electrolysis.

First, the bauxite is processed to get crystals of pure aluminum oxide, called alumina. Alumina melts at a very high temperature, which would be expensive, so it is dissolved at a lower temperature in a molten substance called cryolite. The mixture of alumina and cryolite is put into a container called a cell. The cell is lined with graphite, which forms one of the electrodes. The other electrode, also made of graphite, dips into the mixture from the top. When electricity is passed through the mixture, aluminum ions are attracted to the graphite lining and they turn into aluminum atoms. These atoms group together to form molten aluminum. This is piped off and cooled to form the finished metal.

CHEAP ALUMINUM

Scientists first extracted aluminum in the early 1800s, but only in tiny amounts, and the cost was very high. At the time, aluminum was in short supply and more expensive than gold.

The most important breakthrough in the extraction of aluminum was the invention of the dynamo—a machine that produces electricity. This allowed power stations to be built, providing the electricity needed for the electrolysis of aluminum oxide.

Two scientists, the American Charles Hall and the Frenchman Paul-Louis-Toussaint Héroult, both developed a method of producing aluminum by electrolysis in 1886. Soon aluminum was available in large amounts, and it became much cheaper than gold.

The iron and steel industry

Iron is the cheapest and most useful metal in the world, and steel is its most important alloy. Iron-making and steel-making are two of the world's largest industries, and hundreds of millions of tons of steel are made every year. Here you can find out how iron is extracted from its ore and turned into steel.

Smelting iron

Iron is extracted from its ore, iron oxide, in a very hot furnace called a blast furnace. Iron oxide and coke (which is almost pure carbon) are put into the top of the furnace, and air is blasted into the base of the furnace. The coke does two jobs. First, it burns in the air, heating the furnace to 1,500 °C (2,700 °F). Second, because carbon is more reactive than iron, it displaces the iron from the iron oxide. Here's the equation for the reaction:

$$\text{carbon} + \text{iron oxide} \rightarrow \text{carbon dioxide} + \text{iron}$$
$$3C + 2Fe_2O_3 \rightarrow 3CO_2 + 4Fe$$

The molten iron flows to the bottom of the furnace and through pipes to be collected. It is then put in molds and cooled. The iron from the blast furnace is called pig iron. It contains up to 10 percent carbon, which makes it very brittle.

◀ The scene at a blast furnace. Huge vats of molten metal are handled by remote control.

Iron to steel

Steel is iron that contains about 1 percent carbon. Iron from a blast furnace is made into steel in a basic oxygen furnace. Molten iron is poured into the furnace, then jets of pure oxygen are blown into the iron. The oxygen reacts with the carbon, producing carbon dioxide. This is then removed from the furnace. This reduces the amount of carbon in the iron and produces steel. The furnace is tipped up, and the steel pours into molds to cool. A large steel-making plant can make up to 10 million tons of steel a year, which is enough to make a thousand large cargo ships.

HENRY BESSEMER (1813–1898)

British engineer Henry Bessemer invented the modern steel-making process in the middle of the 1800s. He realized that blowing air through molten iron would remove the carbon from the iron, making steel. Before this, steel was a rare and expensive metal, but afterward it became cheaper and the most widely used metal.

Working with metals

The metal made in most production plants is poured into molds to make lumps called **ingots**. In a steel-making factory, the steel is fed into a machine that shapes it into sheets or bars. This is called continuous casting. Ingots, bars, and sheets of metal are the **raw materials** for making all sorts of objects.

Casting, forging, and rolling

Casting, forging, and rolling are the three main methods of making pieces of metal into different shapes. In casting, the metal is heated until it melts and is then poured into a mold. Inside the mold is a hole the same shape as the object to be cast. The hole fills with metal, which cools to form the object. In forging, the metal is heated until it glows red hot, but not enough to melt it. This makes it more malleable, and it can then be pressed or hammered into shape by machines or by hand tools.

In rolling, slabs of metal travel through a series of rollers that gradually flatten them into thin sheets, or bend them into tubes. Blocks of metal can also be made into shapes with various cutting tools.

A blacksmith bends and shapes iron by heating it
and hitting it with a hammer. This is called forging.

Joining metals

Pieces of metals can be joined together by welding and soldering. In one method of welding, the edges of the pieces are heated until they are so hot that they fuse together. In soldering, used in electronics and plumbing, an alloy called solder is melted so that it flows into the gap between the metals, bonds to them, and joins them together.

Making metal coatings

Many metal objects have a thin coating of another metal on their surfaces. Silverware is often silver-plated, which means it is made of steel with a coating of silver on the outside. Jewelry and ornaments are often gold-plated instead of being solid gold. Metal coatings are normally applied by electrolysis.

Metal recycling

Many metals can be recycled, which means that metal in old or worn-out objects is made into new objects. Recycling not only saves more metal ore from being dug out of the ground, but also saves the energy that would have been used to extract the metal from the ore.

▲ Aluminum cans waiting to be recycled.

METAL FATIGUE

Metal fatigue happens when a piece of metal changes its shape slightly, again and again. This weakens the metal and eventually makes it break. Metal fatigue is a big problem in machines where metal parts, such as springs, are stretched or bent repeatedly. It is difficult to detect, and often parts break suddenly, so it is important that parts of machines such as airplanes are checked regularly for the microscopic cracks that are a sign of metal fatigue.

THE PERIODIC TABLE

The periodic table is a chart of all the known elements. The elements are arranged in order of their atomic numbers, but in rows, so that elements with similar properties are underneath each other. The periodic table gets its name from the fact that the elements' properties repeat themselves every few elements, or periodically. The position of an element in the periodic table gives an idea of what its properties are likely to be.

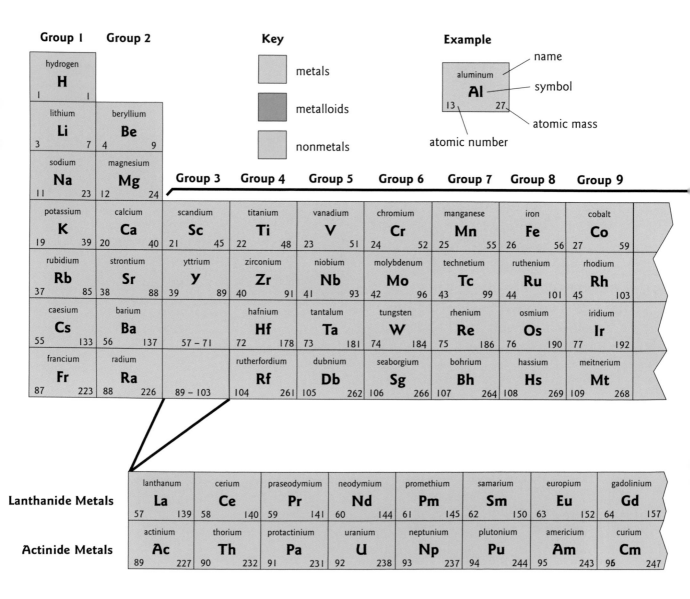

Key

- metals
- metalloids
- nonmetals

Example

aluminum — name
Al — symbol
13 — atomic number
27 — atomic mass

Group 1	Group 2	Group 3	Group 4	Group 5	Group 6	Group 7	Group 8	Group 9
hydrogen **H** 1, 1								
lithium **Li** 3, 7	beryllium **Be** 4, 9							
sodium **Na** 11, 23	magnesium **Mg** 12, 24							
potassium **K** 19, 39	calcium **Ca** 20, 40	scandium **Sc** 21, 45	titanium **Ti** 22, 48	vanadium **V** 23, 51	chromium **Cr** 24, 52	manganese **Mn** 25, 55	iron **Fe** 26, 56	cobalt **Co** 27, 59
rubidium **Rb** 37, 85	strontium **Sr** 38, 88	yttrium **Y** 39, 89	zirconium **Zr** 40, 91	niobium **Nb** 41, 93	molybdenum **Mo** 42, 96	technetium **Tc** 43, 99	ruthenium **Ru** 44, 101	rhodium **Rh** 45, 103
caesium **Cs** 55, 133	barium **Ba** 56, 137	57 – 71	hafnium **Hf** 72, 178	tantalum **Ta** 73, 181	tungsten **W** 74, 184	rhenium **Re** 75, 186	osmium **Os** 76, 190	iridium **Ir** 77, 192
francium **Fr** 87, 223	radium **Ra** 88, 226	89 – 103	rutherfordium **Rf** 104, 261	dubnium **Db** 105, 262	seaborgium **Sg** 106, 266	bohrium **Bh** 107, 264	hassium **Hs** 108, 269	meitnerium **Mt** 109, 268

Lanthanide Metals

lanthanum **La** 57, 139	cerium **Ce** 58, 140	praseodymium **Pr** 59, 141	neodymium **Nd** 60, 144	promethium **Pm** 61, 145	samarium **Sm** 62, 150	europium **Eu** 63, 152	gadolinium **Gd** 64, 157

Actinide Metals

actinium **Ac** 89, 227	thorium **Th** 90, 232	protactinium **Pa** 91, 231	uranium **U** 92, 238	neptunium **Np** 93, 237	plutonium **Pu** 94, 244	americium **Am** 95, 243	curium **Cm** 96, 247

Groups and periods

The vertical columns of elements are called groups. The horizontal rows of elements are called periods. Some groups have special names:

Group 1: Alkali metals
Group 2: Alkaline earth metals
Groups 3–12: Transition metals
Group 17: Halogens
Group 18: Noble gases

The table is divided into two main sections, the metals and nonmetals. Between the two are elements that have some properties of metals and some of nonmetals. They are called semimetals or metalloids.

			Group 13	Group 14	Group 15	Group 16	Group 17	Group 18
								helium **He** 2 4
			boron **B** 5 11	carbon **C** 6 12	nitrogen **N** 7 14	oxygen **O** 8 16	fluorine **F** 9 19	neon **Ne** 10 20
Group 10	Group 11	Group 12	aluminum **Al** 13 27	silicon **Si** 14 28	phosphorus **P** 15 31	sulfur **S** 16 32	chlorine **Cl** 17 35	argon **Ar** 18 40
nickel **Ni** 28 59	copper **Cu** 29 64	zinc **Zn** 30 65	gallium **Ga** 31 70	germanium **Ge** 32 73	arsenic **As** 33 75	selenium **Se** 34 79	bromine **Br** 35 80	krypton **Kr** 36 84
palladium **Pd** 46 106	silver **Ag** 47 108	cadmium **Cd** 48 112	indium **In** 49 115	tin **Sn** 50 119	antimony **Sb** 51 122	tellurium **Te** 52 128	iodine **I** 53 127	xenon **Xe** 54 131
platinum **Pt** 78 195	gold **Au** 79 197	mercury **Hg** 80 201	thallium **Tl** 81 204	lead **Pb** 82 207	bismuth **Bi** 83 209	polonium **Po** 84 209	astatine **At** 85 210	radon **Rn** 86 222
darmstadtium **Ds** 110 281	roentgenium **Rg** 111 272	ununbium **Uub** 112 285	ununtrium **Uut** 113 284	ununquadium **Uuq** 114 289	ununpentium **Uup** 115 288	ununhexium **Uuh** 116 292		

terbium **Tb** 65 159	dysprosium **Dy** 66 163	holmium **Ho** 67 165	erbium **Er** 68 167	thulium **Tm** 69 169	ytterbium **Yb** 70 173	lutetium **Lu** 71 175
berkelium **Bk** 97 247	californium **Cf** 98 251	einsteinium **Es** 99 252	fermium **Fm** 100 257	mendelevium **Md** 101 258	nobelium **No** 102 259	lawrencium **Lr** 103 262

Common metals and metalloids

These are some of the melting and boiling points for pure metals and metalloids that occur in the periodic table.

Metal	Symbol	State at room temperature	Melting pt °C (°F)	Boiling pt °C (°F)
lithium	Li	solid	180 (356)	1,342 (2,448)
sodium	Na	solid	98 (208)	883 (1,621)
magnesium	Mg	solid	650 (1,202)	1,090 (1,994)
aluminum	Al	solid	660 (1,220)	2,519 (4,566)
silicon	Si	solid	1,414 (2,577)	2,900 (5,252)
potassium	K	solid	63 (145)	759 (1,398)
calcium	Ca	solid	842 (1,548)	1,487 (2,709)
iron	Fe	solid	1,535 (2,795)	2,861 (5,182)
copper	Cu	solid	1,083 (1,981)	2,595 (4,703)
zinc	Zn	solid	420 (788)	907 (1,665)
silver	Ag	solid	961 (1,762)	2,210 (4,010)
tin	Sn	solid	232 (450)	2,270 (4,118)
gold	Au	solid	1,063 (1,954)	2,970 (5,378)
mercury	Hg	liquid	-39 (-38)	357 (675)
lead	Pb	solid	327 (621)	1,744 (3,171)

The reactivity series

The reactivity series is a list of common metals in order of their reactivity, together with their reactions with air, water, and acid. The most reactive metals are at the top and least reactive at the bottom.

Metal	Symbol	Air	Water	Acid
potassium	K	Burns easily	Reacts with cold water	Violent reaction
sodium	Na	Burns easily	Reacts with cold water	Violent reaction
calcium	Ca	Burns easily	Reacts with cold water	Violent reaction
magnesium	Mg	Burns easily	Reacts with steam	Very reactive
aluminum	Al	Reacts slowly	Reacts with steam	Very reactive
zinc	Zn	Reacts slowly	Reacts with steam	Quite reactive
iron	Fe	Reacts slowly	Reacts with steam	Quite reactive
lead	Pb	Reacts slowly	Reacts slowly with steam	Reacts very slowly
copper	Cu	Reacts slowly	No reaction	No reaction
silver	Ag	No reaction	No reaction	No reaction
gold	Au	No reaction	No reaction	No reaction

Uses of metals

This list shows the main uses of some common metals. They are in the order that they appear in the periodic table.

Metals	Uses
lithium (Li)	alloys for aircraft manufacture, batteries
magnesium (Mg)	emergency flares and fireworks, alloys for aircraft and car parts
aluminum (Al)	aircraft manufacture, engineering, soda cans, aluminum foil and containers, cookware, telescope mirrors
titanium (Ti)	artificial hip parts, fighter aircraft parts
chromium (Cr)	alloys such as stainless steel, plating, added to glass to give color, catalyst
iron (Fe)	manufacture of steel, engineering and building, ornaments, tools, machine parts
nickel (Ni)	coins, corrosion-resistant alloys, magnets, stainless steel, batteries
copper (Cu)	coins, electrical cables, tracks on electronic circuit boards, water pipes and tubing, roofing and weatherproofing, alloys such as brass
zinc (Zn)	batteries, galvanization of iron and steel (for rust protection), alloys such as brass, electric fuses
silver (Ag)	coins, jewelry and silverware, silver plating, electronic components, wire, dental alloys, batteries
tin (Sn)	solder, plating inside food cans, alloys
platinum (Pt)	jewelry, wire, electrical contacts, catalyst
gold (Au)	jewelry and ornaments, gold plating of ornaments, dentistry, electrical contacts
mercury (Hg)	thermometers, barometers, electronic tilt switches, mercury vapor lamps, batteries
lead (Pb)	batteries, building waterproofing and roofing, solder, radiation protection

GLOSSARY OF TECHNICAL TERMS

acid liquid that is sour to taste, that can eat away metals, and is neutralized by alkalis and bases. Acids have a pH below 7.

alkali liquid with a pH above 7. Alkalis feel soapy and slimy.

alloy material made by mixing a metal with another metal or a small amount of a nonmetal. For example, steel is an alloy of iron and carbon.

atom extremely tiny particle of matter. The smallest particle of an element that can exist, and which has the properties of that element. All substances are made up of atoms.

boiling point temperature at which a substance changes state from liquid to gas

bond connection between two atoms, ions, or molecules

catalyst chemical that makes a chemical reaction happen faster but is itself unchanged at the end of the reaction

charge electricity on an object, such as an atom or electron

chemical reaction happens when two chemicals (called the reactants) react together to form new chemicals (called the products)

compound substance that contains two or more different elements joined together by chemical bonds

conductor material that allows electricity (an electrical conductor) or heat (a heat conductor) to pass through it easily

corrosion any chemical reaction that eats away a material, such as rusting

decompose turn into more simple chemicals

density amount of a substance (or mass) in a certain volume. Density is measured in ounces per cubic inch or pounds per cubic yard.

ductile material that can be pulled into a thin wire without breaking. Metals are ductile.

electrode solid electrical conductor, usually graphite or metal, that is in contact with the liquid in electrolysis

electron extremely tiny particle that is part of an atom. Electrons are negatively charged, and they move around the nucleus of an atom.

element substance that contains just one type of atom. An element cannot be changed into simpler substances.

extract remove a substance from a mixture of substances

galvanizing coating iron or steel objects with a layer of zinc to keep them from rusting

geological survey investigation to find out which layers of rocks are under the ground in a particular place

ingot piece of pure metal, such as gold, made by pouring molten metal into a mold

magnetic material that is attracted to a magnet or can be turned into a magnet itself

malleable material that can be hammered into shape without breaking. All metals are malleable.

melting point temperature at which a substance changes state from a solid to a liquid as it warms up

metal any element in the periodic table that is shiny, and that conducts electricity and heat well. Most metals are also hard.

metalloid element that cannot be classed as a metal or a nonmetal. It has some of the properties of a metal and some of the properties of a nonmetal.

mixture substance made up of two or more elements or compounds that are not joined together by chemical bonds

molten substance that has been heated until it melts

native metal metal that is found as an element in Earth's crust rather than as part of a compound. Gold is a native metal.

neutron one of the particles that makes up the nucleus of an atom. Neutrons are not electrically charged.

nonmetal any element in the periodic table that is not a metal. Most nonmetals are gases.

nucleus central part of an atom

ore material dug from the ground that contains useful elements, such as iron, aluminum, or sulfur

oxide compound made up of a metal or nonmetal combined with oxygen, such as aluminum oxide or carbon dioxide

particle very tiny piece of a substance, such as a single atom, ion, or molecule

product substance formed during a chemical reaction

properties characteristics of a chemical, such as color, feel, and density

proton one of the particles that makes up the nucleus of an atom. Protons are positively charged.

radiation rays, such as light and heat, or streams of particles

radioactive substance that gives off radiation

raw material simple material that is made into more complex materials or objects

reactant substance that takes part in a chemical reaction

reactive chemical that takes part in chemical reactions easily

solution liquid made when a substance (the solute) dissolves in a liquid (the solvent)

trend general direction of change in a property

X-ray form of radiation that passes through some substances (such as flesh), but not others (such as bone)

FURTHER READING

Baldwin, Carol. *Metals*. Chicago: Heinemann Raintree, 2006.

e. science encyclopedia. New York: DK Publishing, 2004.

Parsons, Jayne. *The Way Science Works*. New York: DK Publishing, 2002.

Useful websites

http://www.billnye.com
Includes a number of physical science experiments designed to do at home.
http://www.chemicalelements.com
An interactive Periodic table. Originally created, in 1996, as an 8th grade science project.

http://www.chem4kids.com
A lot of information and activities on chemistry, presented in a fun way.
http://www.creative-chemistry.org.uk
An interactive chemistry site including fun practical activities, worksheets, quizzes, puzzles, and more!
http://www.heinemannexplore.com
An online resource for school libraries and classrooms containing articles, investigations, biographies, and activities related to all areas of the science curriculum.
http://www.webelements.com/webelements/scholar
The Periodic table – online! Discover more about all the elements and their properties.

Experiment results:

page 11: The magnet will pick up the iron nails but not the copper nails. This shows that the iron nails are magnetic.

page 13: The pea on the metal spoon is the first to fall because the heat from the water spreads more quickly through the metal than through the plastic. This shows that metals are better conductors of heat.

page 23: Each of the metals you tested will be covered with a layer of a new substance. This is probably an oxide of the metal, formed by the reaction of the metal with oxygen in the air. The aluminum reacted most quickly, followed by iron and then copper.

page 25: After a few minutes, the nail begins to fizz. These bubbles are hydrogen being formed by the reaction between the zinc and the acid. When the fizzing stops, all the zinc has finished reacting, and a plain steel nail is left.

page 29: The only nail to rust is the one in jar 1, which was exposed to both air and water. This means that both water and air are necessary for steel to rust.

INDEX